# The Hunter's Dream

## Meja Mwangi

**The Hunter's Dream**

© Copyright text M. Mwangi 1993
© Copyright illustrations Macmillan Education Ltd 1993

All rights reserved. No reproduction, copy or transmission of this publication may be made without written permission.

No paragraph of this publication may be reproduced, copied or transmitted save with written permission or in accordance with the provisions of the Copyright, Designs and Patents Act 1988, or under the terms of any licence permitting limited copying issued by the Copyright Licensing Agency, 90 Tottenham Court Road, London W1P 9HE.

Any person who does any unauthorised act in relation to this publication may be liable to criminal prosecution and civil claims for damages.

First published 1993 by
MACMILLAN EDUCATION LTD
London and Basingstoke
*Associated companies and representatives in Accra, Banjul, Cairo, Dar es Salaam, Delhi, Freetown, Gaborone, Harare, Hong Kong, Johannesburg, Kampala, Lagos, Lahore, Lusaka, Mexico City, Nairobi, São Paulo, Tokyo*

ISBN 0–333–58002–8

12  11  10  9   8   7   6   5   4   3
06  05  04  03  02  01  00  99  98  97

Printed in Hong Kong


A catalogue record for this book is available from the British Library.


*Series editor: Lorna Evans*


*Illustrations by Meshack Asare*

# Chapter 1

Once there was a man who was poor. He had one wife, no friends, no neighbours and no children. He had three cows, three goats and three hens. He had no money. He was so poor that he only had one name. His name was Kori.

Kori and his wife lived on the far side of the hills. And because they had no friends, no neighbours and no children their life was hard.

Kori and his wife wished to have a child. For many years they prayed for one.

Every morning Kori said,

"If God will send us a child our days will be full of light."

And every morning his wife added,

"And our lives will be happy for ever."

Kori made sacrifices to God. He begged the spirits of his ancestors for help. He left fruits and wild honey and beads and stones under the sacred trees.

But the prayers of Kori and his wife were not answered. No child came.

So after many years of prayers Kori said to his wife,

"God does not wish to give us a child. I shall not ask again. I shall make no more sacrifices. My prayers for a child have ended."

Kori's wife still wanted a child more than anything.

"What are you saying to me?" she cried. "I want a child, I tell you. I want a child to help me. I want a child to fetch water from the river. I want a child to work in the fields. I want a child to watch over the cows and the goats."

Kori answered, "God does not wish to give us a child. We can do no more."

"But husband, I am tired of being alone. I want a child. I want a child to work with me and stay with me when you are away."

"Be quiet," Kori told his wife. "Your words will not help us. Your words will bring only pain and sadness."

But Kori's wife would not be quiet.

"Why can you not give me a child?" she cried. "Why must I wait? Why are you not a real husband to me? Why are you not a real man?"

The words cut Kori like a sharp knife, and still his wife would not be quiet.

"Do you not want a second name?" she shouted, so loudly that all the birds flew up from the trees.

For a few seconds Kori stood still as a stone, not moving, not speaking. Every man wanted a second name. Then at last he spoke.

"Do not say these things," he said sadly. "I have no second name. I shall wait for a second name as I have waited for a child."

Kori's wife saw how she hurt him, but still she went on.

"If you were a real man you would give me a child," she screamed. "Then your wait would be over."

Kori's wife ran into the hut and would not come out. For days she would not talk to him. Sometimes he heard her singing softly to herself,

"I cry no tear
For want of a deer,
I want a child near
For ever to hold dear."

Kori was sad. He did not know what to do. At last he picked up his spear and his arrows and went out into the wild forest.

He was gone for many, many days.

When he came home he was carrying a large load on his back. The load was heavy, and Kori was bent low under it.

"Wife, come out. I have something for you," he called loudly, dropping his load in the dust.

Kori's wife heard him and ran out of the hut. She looked at the load. What could it be? It was long and round, and Kori had tied banana leaves around it.

"I have something for you," he said to her again.

Kori watched his wife as her long fingers pulled away the banana leaves. Her face lit up and her eyes were smiling at last.

But as the last leaf fell and Kori's wife saw what was inside she turned away from him.

"Stop," Kori cried. "See what I have brought for you. Honey. Wild honey. I took it, drop by drop, from the

3

trees. I have brought you the best honey, the sweetest honey, from the forest."

"I do not want it," was all that his wife said, and she went back into the hut. She lay down on a mat, and she would not talk to him for many days.

All the time Kori could hear her singing to herself,
> "I cry no tear
> For want of deer.
> I want a child near
> For ever to hold dear."

# Chapter 2

Kori was sad and unhappy and he still wanted a child just as much as his wife.

He prayed to God again. He took one of his hens and sacrificed it under a sacred tree. He prayed and prayed, but no child came.

He took his second hen to a second sacred tree and prayed once more. No child came.

Kori took his third hen to a third sacred tree, and again he prayed. Still God did not answer his prayers, for no child came.

One by one Kori took all his animals to the sacred trees. He sacrificed his goats and two of his milk cows, and said a thousand more prayers.

Still there was no child.

Now Kori and his wife had only one milk cow left.

"I shall not sacrifice this last cow," said Kori. "Do not ask that of me, for I cannot do it."

Kori's wife said nothing. She just sang softly,
"I cry no tear
For want of a deer.
I want a child near
For ever to hold dear."

"I tried," said Kori softly. "You know I tried."

Then came the great drought.

Every day the sun rode high in a bright blue sky. Every day a few thin clouds followed in its path. Every day the people waited for rain.

But no rain fell.

Once the river was a mile wide, full and fast. Now it was a narrow stream, slow and brown.

Once the forests were thick with great green trees and flowers of red and blue. Now they were dull and dusty, bare and ugly.

Once the crops grew tall and thick in the fields. Now they were burnt orange and dry by the sun.

Soon there was no food. Everybody was hungry. Kori's wife cried great tears.

"Why must I be hungry," she said. "Why can you not grow food for me? Why are you so poor? Why do you not look after your wife?"

"These are hard times," Kori answered. "Everybody is hungry. Everybody wants food. Hard times come and go. But remember, wife, that we are nothing without God."

Kori was right, but his wife would not listen to him.

People ate anything that they could find, and still they were hungry. Even the wild animals could not be caught. They learned to run fast and hide away from the hunters. Only a very good hunter could catch them.

Kori was the best hunter of them all. He was tall and strong, and afraid of nothing. His ancestors were the Dorobo, who were the greatest hunters ever known. No animal, big or small, was safe from the Dorobo. They were the bravest people who ever lived.

The Dorobo were hunters, but they also took the wild fruit and nuts and honey from the forests.

All through the awful years of the drought Kori and his wife lived on deer meat and wild honey. Kori followed the deer through the thickest forest for day after day until his arrow or his spear could do its work. He never went home without something to eat.

But his wife was never happy.

"Why do you not bring me more food?" she said.


One night Kori had a dream. He dreamed that he travelled many miles to a far away place. In the place of

his dream the wind blew gently and the rain fell each day. There was no drought.

In the place of Kori's dream the crops grew tall in the farmer's fields. The wild animals had no fear of men, and would eat from the hand. There was always food and no child cried from hunger.

In the place of Kori's dream men and women lived happily together. There was no sadness, and dreams came true.

The next day Kori told his dream to his wife.
His wife laughed at him and said,
"You foolish man. You know that your dreams can never come true."

"This one will," Kori told her. "I shall leave you now. I shall find the place of my dream. I shall never give up. And one day I shall bring you a child, a child who will light up your life. Then you will be happy for ever."

Kori's wife just laughed again.

"Before I go," Kori went on, "I must do one more thing."

And saying that he took a rope and tied it round the neck of his last milk cow.

"A time comes when even the best of friends must leave each other. Such a time is now. Let us pray that we shall both be better for this," he said sadly.

Kori's wife watched as he led the cow away.

"I am sad to do this," she heard him say, "but I would give all the cows that ever lived for a child."

With these words Kori left home.

Kori's wife listened as the cow followed Kori away. She listened for a long time, and then she could hear nothing more.

# Chapter
# | 3 |

Kori travelled far and wide. He travelled through the forests and on to places where no trees grew. He travelled over the hills and down into the valleys. He walked many miles to find the place of his dream.

After many days and many weeks Kori came to a river. It was wide and long, dark and very deep. Its waters were so slow that it was almost a sea.

Kori stood quite still and looked across the river. On the far side there were thousands and thousands of deer, zebra, wildebeeste and other animals. They were eating the rich green grass that grew among the bushes and under the trees. There was no drought or hunger there.

Kori knew at once where he was. This was the place of his dream. He had found the place where dreams come true.

"I must cross the river," Kori said softly to himself. There was nobody to hear him.

"I must cross the river," he said again.

But there was no bridge across the river. What was Kori to do?

Kori took the rope from the neck of his cow. Perhaps she was thirsty and wanted to drink. Then he sat down to think. He thought and thought. He thought so hard and he was so tired that at last he fell fast asleep.

He slept for a long time. Then suddenly there was a great noise, like a tree falling into a river. Kori jumped to his feet. He did not really know what he was doing. What was happening? Where was he?

Kori looked across the river. He closed his eyes and

then opened them again. He still thought that he might be dreaming.

A huge black serpent was crossing the river. Slowly, almost lazily, it came towards Kori. Then it lifted itself out of the water and lay on the grass.

The serpent was so long that it took all day to slip out of the river, rolling and turning. Even then there were miles and miles of it still in the water.

The serpent lay by the river to sun itself. Kori ran forward, spear in hand, to stand between the serpent and his cow.

The serpent looked up and saw Kori.

"Who are you?" it hissed. "What do you want from the River of Hope?"

Kori tried to smile as he answered the serpent.

"I am a poor man from far away. I wish to cross the River of Hope."

"Nobody can cross the River of Hope unless I let him" the serpent hissed. "Once every three years I wait here until somebody comes, wishing to cross. Why do you wish to cross the River of Hope, poor man from far away?"

Kori spoke again to the serpent.

"My wife begs me to give her a child," he answered. "Day after day she cries. Day after day she prays. Her prayers are always the same. I am looking for a child for my wife."

The serpent listened to Kori's words.

"Give me your spear," it hissed. "Then I may help you to cross the River of Hope."

Kori's spear was his right arm. It was his strength and his life. He could not live without it.

"I cannot give you my spear," he answered.

"Then give me your arrows. You can live without your arrows," the serpent hissed.

The arrows were Kori's left arm. They were his meat and his honey. He could not live without them.

"I cannot give you my arrows," he told the serpent.

"Then I will take your cow," the serpent hissed. "She is thin and old and ugly. You can live without your cow."

"No," Kori cried. "I am only a poor man. I have no money. I have only this cow to buy my wife a child."

The serpent was getting angry.

"You must give me something. Nothing will come from nothing," it told Kori.

Kori knew that the serpent was right, and he knew something else too. He knew that if he could cross the River of Hope, he would be in the place of his dream. There he would not need money. There he would not need his cow. There he could have anything he wished for.

"You may take my cow," he said, standing aside. "But serpent, listen to me. You must do as you say. You must let me cross the River of Hope. You must not trick me. If you break your word, you will be sorry."

The serpent took the cow, smiling to itself. It turned its thick black body in great circles around the poor animal. The cow slipped along the serpent's body down to its home, deep in the water of the River of Hope.

This took a long long time, for the serpent was longer than a long long day.

# Chapter 4

Then the huge black serpent rolled and turned and pulled itself across the water. It touched both sides of the River of Hope, like a bridge.

"Why do you wish to cross the river, poor man from far away?" the serpent asked Kori again.

"Because I want to go to the place of my dream," Kori answered. "Because I want to go to the place where wishes come true."

"But you are there already. You are in the place where wishes come true."

"I am not," Kori told the serpent. "You cannot trick me. I am in a place of sadness. I am in a place where rain never falls. I am in a place where old men are

hungry and children die because there is no food. I must cross the River of Hope to find the place where dreams come true."

"And I am telling you, you are in that place," hissed the serpent.

Kori looked around. He was still in the same place, the place by the river where he had fallen asleep. Nothing had changed – but his cow was now in the serpent's home, deep in the water of the River of Hope.

He got very angry and holding his spear high above his head he shouted out loud,
"Do you think I am a fool? Do you think you can trick me? Why are you doing this to me?"

"Look around you," hissed the serpent. "Look around."

Kori did as the serpent told him, but he was still in the place by the river where he had fallen asleep.

"I am not a fool," he shouted, beside himself with anger now. "I know where I am. No dream ever came true here. This is a place of sadness. This is a place of hunger and drought. I know it well. I have always lived in such a place."

"If you say so, then must it be so," the serpent hissed.

"Take me across the water now," Kori screamed, not listening to the serpent. "Take me now, I tell you. No more tricks. I have paid you well. Take me across the River of Hope."

The serpent did not say another word, but rolled the circles of its great black body across the water.

"Climb on my body," it told Kori, and as Kori did so it lifted him high in the air. Kori slid down the serpent's body and fell heavily on the grass on the far side of the River of Hope.

He rolled over and over, and then lay quite still.

Then Kori opened his eyes. He got to his feet. He looked around.

What had happened? He had crossed the River of Hope on the serpent's body – or had he?

Kori looked again. He thought he was in the very same place that he had just left. The river was the same. The grass was the same. Every tree was the same. Every hill was the same. Kori could remember it all. Everything looked just the same as on the other side.

"What is happening? What have you done? Why am I here?" he asked the serpent.

"I told you, I told you," the serpent hissed.

"That is no answer," Kori shouted, angry again. "You tricked me. Give me back my cow. I want my cow, now, at once. If you do not give me my cow you will be sorry. You will eat my spear and my arrow will find a home in your body."

"I cannot give you back your cow," hissed the serpent. "Once given, nothing can be taken back. You know that, poor man from far away."

Kori lifted his spear.

"I want my cow back. You did not keep your word."

"You wanted to cross the River of Hope."

"Yes, to the other side," Kori shouted.

"But you are on the other side now."

"No, I am not on the other side. Take me across or I will kill you."

The serpent looked coldly at Kori.

"I am tired of you," it hissed. "You know nothing. Keep your angry words to yourself."

Kori did not hear the serpent.

"Give me back my cow. Take me to the other side of the River of Hope," he shouted again and again.

"You are on the other side," hissed the serpent. "Now listen to me, for this is the last time that I shall speak to you. I brought you over from the other side. You wanted to follow your dream, and I did as you asked. Take your dream if you can find it, poor man from far away."

And saying this the huge black serpent rolled lazily away and slipped into the deep brown water of the River of Hope.

Kori was alone, and so angry that he could not speak. The serpent had tricked him, he knew that. The serpent had tricked him, and now it had gone. What had it said? It waited every three years by the River of Hope? He could not wait that long.

Somehow Kori could hear his wife speaking. He could hear her words.

"Dreams never come true," she would say. "You are a fool, husband. Dreams never come true."

Kori knew that he could not go home.

# Chapter
# | 5 |

Kori travelled on for many days and many nights. He went over the hills and down into the valleys. He travelled into the dark forests and open fields. He travelled to places where rain never fell. He travelled to places where the wind never blew.

Kori travelled to places where a day's work lasted for ever. He travelled to places where singing was never heard and dancing was never seen.

He travelled for a long, long time. He looked everywhere. But he never again found the River of Hope or the huge black serpent or the place of his dream.

In the very last place of all, the place where the sun never smiled down from the sky, Kori stopped.

He waited for three days, because he did not know what to do next. Should he go on? Should he give up? Should he go back to his wife? Would she take him back into her hut?

"I told you so, you fool." He could hear her laughing at him across the miles. "I told you so. Dreams never come true. Never. Not here. Not there. Not anywhere."

Perhaps Kori's wife was right, but Kori did not think so. After all, he had found the River of Hope. Perhaps he had even found the place of his dreams, although he had not known it.

Night found him still waiting. It was cold and windy, colder and windier than he had ever known before. The wind chased through the grass. It carried the sharp smell of the wild dogs hiding nearby. It swept up the dry leaves and drove them through the air.

The moon came up from behind the hills, hard and

silvery. In its light Kori saw zebra hiding among the bushes. He saw deer and gazelle and a hundred other animals. Kori wished that he could be like them, no homes, no wives and no dreams to think about.

In the middle of the night the wind dropped. Kori fell into a deep sleep, and dreamed of serpents, huge and black. He dreamed of drought and hunger, and saw the bodies of the birds and animals that had died. He dreamed of anger and hurt. He came face to face with pain.

There were great storms in the air. The sun fought with the moon, and there were wars in the sky.

As Kori watched the sun crashed against the silvery moon. The moon broke into a thousand tiny parts, and they fell like feathers. Then all the stars cried out and there was a sadness that had never been known before.

Kori had many dreams that night, but this was the worst of all.

Kori did not know when morning came, in that place where the sun never smiled. When he opened his eyes and looked up there was no moon in the sky. But when he looked again he saw a small silvery light, far far away. He knew at once that his dream had come true. The moon had been broken.

Kori picked up his spear and his arrows and ran to the silver light, to the place where the moon might have fallen. He travelled for many hours.

But when Kori came to the silvery light he was afraid. He stood and watched it, not touching or even going near to it.

For the silvery light was not the moon at all. It was a huge, round thing, much larger than the largest egg. It lay in a nest of sticks and leaves, high up in an old, bent tree. Kori could just see it from where he stood. He could even feel its warmth on his face.

"A moon egg," Kori said softly. "A moon egg. How beautiful it is."

The nest in which the moon egg lay was the nest of a weaver bird. There were thousands of those nests in the old bent tree, nest after nest after nest. Kori thought that there was a whole city of nests in the tree.

But although there were so many nests, Kori could not see any weaver birds. He could not hear them either. Where were they? Had they left their nests? Were they all asleep?

Kori put his spear and his arrows against the foot of the tree and began to climb. It was hard, but he went on, higher and higher. Somehow he knew that he had to get to the moon egg before anything else did.

At last he came close to the moon egg and put out his hand to touch it. It was soft and smooth. As he touched it he felt its warmth pass through his fingers and along his arm, into his cold body and even down to his toes. He was filled with its warmth.

"This is the most beautiful thing I have ever seen," he said to himself. "What would my wife have to say about this?"

Saying this, he lifted up the moon egg and put it into his bag. Then he climbed down the tree, picked up his spear and his arrows, and turned away.

Then suddenly the tree came alive. And not just the old bent tree, but every other tree for miles around.

Weaver birds screamed out of their nests and took to the air. Calling out loud they chased after Kori. He saw them coming and started to run. Faster and faster he ran, but it was no good. He could not get away. A thousand weaver birds were chasing him, and then a thousand more.

Kori ran as he had never run before.

## Chapter 6

Kori crashed through bushes and trees, but it was no good. He could not get away from the screaming weaver birds.

They filled the air until the sky was black. They flew around him in a thousand circles, until their wings brushed against his face. They screamed out loud until he could hear nothing else.

Kori ran on, his arms above his head to keep the birds away. Still they came after him, their sharp beaks digging deep into his back. The pain was so great that Kori thought his body was on fire.

Kori tried to drive them away, but the weaver birds were not afraid of him. He screamed for help, time after time, but there was nobody to hear him.

The birds chased Kori all day. He kept up his fight with them, hitting out when he could, and kicking with his feet. Sometimes Kori hurt one of them. Sometimes one dropped dead from the sky. But still they came after him.

Then, as suddenly as they had come, the weaver birds went away. Their screams stopped. They flew high into the air, turned and made their way home.

Kori stopped running and listened. He could hear nothing. He looked up into the sky and saw the stars. Night had fallen. Too tired to even think, Kori lay down and slept.

Next morning Kori did not know whether it had all been an awful dream, or whether he really had fought the weaver birds.

He did not know until he felt his own body. He hurt all over. The sharp beaks of the weaver birds had cut him a hundred times. So it was real, he told himself. The fight had happened.

Kori suddenly remembered the moon egg. He felt in his leather bag. It was safe!

Kori felt very happy, and then something else happened. He knew where he was. He was sitting in one of his own fields. He was home.

"I'm home," he cried. He did not know whether anybody heard him. He just had to shout out the words, "I'm home."

Kori jumped to his feet and ran to find his wife. He ran over to the hut.

"Wife, I'm here. It's me, your husband, Kori. I'm home."

Kori's wife did not answer.

"Wife, I'm home. I've come home."

Still there was no answer.

Kori pushed open the door of his wife's hut. It was dark inside, but he could just see his wife. She lay on a grass mat by a dead fire, thin and tired and old. She was waiting to die from hunger.

"What have you brought?" she asked. Kori could only just hear her.

"What have you brought?" she asked again, very softly. "I am so hungry I could eat a child."

"I did not find a child," Kori told her.

"Then why did you come back?" she asked.

"I found something else. Something for which I paid very dearly."

"Show me," said his wife.

So Kori took the moon egg out of his leather bag and held it out to her. It lay in his hands, silvery in the darkness of the hut.

"This is the most beautiful thing I have ever seen," Kori said. "This is the softest, warmest thing I have ever touched. Come, wife. Touch it. Hold it yourself."

"I do not want to hold it," his wife told him, very angry. "I want to eat it. Cook it at once, for my hunger cannot wait."

Kori shook his head. He knew he could not do that. He did not know why, but he knew he had to save the moon egg.

"We must not eat it," he said to his wife. "The weaver birds fought hard for it. Who knows, out of it may come a hundred birds. We would all be better for it."

"You old fool," his wife said, even more angrily. "A hundred birds? I say a hundred snakes. Break it open at once and let us see what lies inside."

"If we break it open it will die," Kori said. "We must not kill what is inside. The birds fought too bravely for that."

"You love that egg more than you love your wife." Kori's wife started to cry. "From now on I have no husband and I am not your wife. I shall die of hunger and you will do nothing to help."

Kori did not want his wife to die. He took his arrows and his spear and went out to hunt.

While Kori was out of the hut, his wife started to think. The egg was like no egg she had ever seen before. Perhaps Kori was right. Perhaps they should not eat it.

Somehow she made her way to the moon egg and picked it up. She touched it with her long fingers. At once its warmth ran through her arms and into her body.

She sat on a mat, running her fingers softly over the moon egg. As she did so she thought of the child she had never had, and how she would have loved it.

"How I wish I had a child," she said to herself over and over again. "How I wish I had a child."

# Chapter
| 7 |

When Kori came back, with deer meat in his leather bag, his wife was sitting quietly. She held the silvery moon egg in her hands, and there was a far-away look in her eyes. She was smiling. Kori was glad to see this, for his wife did not often smile.

Kori touched his wife's hand.

"I have killed a deer. Light the fire, wife. Let us eat, for we are both hungry."

Kori's wife put the mooon egg down on a mat by the wall of the hut and started her work. She did not speak to Kori, and he said nothing more to her.

Kori's wife cooked the deer meat and they ate. After that they fell into a deep, deep sleep.

But Kori's sleep was not quiet, for awful dreams filled his head. He dreamed that the moon egg was cold.

"I am cold," the moon egg said to him. "Bring me near to the warmth of the fire."

In the dream, Kori's wife picked up the moon egg and brought it to the fire. As she put it down it slipped out of her hands and broke on the fire stones. Out of the moon egg came a crow, a weaver bird and a butterfly. One by one they flew away.

Kori told his wife about the dream later.

"It was a bad dream, a very bad dream. You will do something for which I shall always be sorry. Not today. Not tomorrow. But one day you will do an awful thing and I shall always be sorry."

"You and your dreams," was all that Kori's wife said.

Later Kori went into the forest with his spear and his arrows and caught a big fat gazelle. He took the fat from its body, and boiled it in a small pot. Then he saved the fat in a bigger pot, and let it cool.

When the fat had cooled it was thick and yellow. Kori added wild honey to the fat, until it was beautifully soft. Then he put the moon egg into the pot and left it near the fire.

From that day Kori had no more bad dreams.

Life went on. Kori's days were filled with hunting. His wife cooked the deer meat and looked after the hut and the moon egg.

When Kori looked into the pot some days later the moon egg was much bigger than when he first found it. It was still soft and warm and silvery.

Again Kori went into the forest with his spear and his arrows. He caught a second fat gazelle. Again he took the fat from its body, boiled it and added wild honey. By now the big pot was nearly full.

Still the moon egg grew and grew.

Kori's wife brought more and more wood and the fire never went out in the hut. They took it in turns to keep it burning through the nights.

And still the moon egg grew and grew. It grew large and round and fat. Kori and his wife grew thin and tired from working for it.

One day Kori's wife said,

"Why are we doing this? Everything we do is for this egg. All the fat meat is for the egg. All the wild honey is for the egg. I have never worked so hard before. And I do not even know what I am working for. Why are we doing all this work for the egg?"

"We must wait," Kori told her. "I do not know what we wait for, but we must wait."

"Wait, wait, work, work. I'm tired of it, I tell you," Kori's wife shouted. "Well I'm not going to work any more."

From that day on Kori looked after the moon egg himself. He watched the fire all night so that it did not go out. He fetched wood in the morning so that the fire would burn brightly all day. He hunted in the forest for gazelle. He found wild honey in the trees. He fed the moon egg every day. He was never tired of looking after it.

After many days Kori saw a tiny crack in the moon egg. The crack got bigger and bigger. Suddenly it cracked wide open. Out of the moon egg came a long black serpent with eyes as red as fire. It hissed angrily at Kori's wife, then slipped out of the door and away into the forest.

Next, out of the moon egg, came a small black crow with a beak as red as fire. It screamed loudly at Kori's wife before flying out of the hut and up into the sky.

And last, out of the moon egg, came a baby, the most beautiful baby ever seen. Kori lifted the baby in his arms, and saw that it was a girl. Her skin was black as night. Her hair was soft and fine. Her round eyes were like stars, dancing with light.

"All my dreams have come true," Kori said to himself, smiling. "I shall never wish for anything else as long as I live."

Then he gave the child to his wife.

"Here," he said. "Here is the child you have waited for. Take her and love her, for she is yours. She will light up your life and you will be happy for ever."

Kori's wife took the baby in her arms. She could not speak. She had never felt such happiness. She carried the baby outside. She showed her to the trees and the flowers and the butterflies and birds and all the other beautiful things.

"Look," she called out loud for all to hear. "Look at my child. Has such beauty ever been seen before?"

The trees and flowers and butterflies and birds made no answer, for truly this was the most beautiful child.

The baby smiled up at the sun in her own shy way. When Kori and his wife gave her a name they called her Thoni, the shy one.

# Chapter
# | 8 |

Kori's wife looked after the child. She was happy now. She laughed and smiled all day long.

"Kori," she said to him, "now I can truly call you My Husband."

So now Kori had a second name, but it was not the best name that he had. The best name was the one which Thoni gave him when she learned to speak. Her very first word was "Father."

When she said that it was the happiest day of Kori's life.

Thoni was the dearest of all children. As she grew up, her beauty grew too. Soon everybody knew of her and spoke of her. People came from far and near to see her and talk with her. She brought happiness to all.

Thoni always wanted to help, but she wanted to help so much that she often did things wrong.

Sometimes she would run down to the river for water. Then when she came to the water she would stop and say,

"Why am I here? What am I doing by the river?"

Sometimes she would go into the forest for wood. Then she would walk among the trees asking,

"Why did I come here? What do I want in the forest?"

Thoni often forgot what she was doing, and she often made mistakes too. She could never mend her own clothes. She was afraid of fire, so she never learned how to cook. She could never sweep the dust from the floor away cleanly. It always blew all over the hut.

Thoni was good at one thing, and one thing alone. When she was little more than a baby she could weave. Soon she could weave better than anyone else.

Tall grass grew in a corner of her mother's yard. This grass was all that Thoni needed. If she cut the grass one morning, she always found more the next day.

With the grass Thoni wove beautiful baskets and mats. Soon everybody heard about her weaving. People came from far and near to watch her and speak with her.

"How beautiful," they said, looking at her face.

"How beautiful," they said, looking at her mats.

People always bought things before they left. They bought thousands of Thoni's baskets. They bought thousands of her mats. They bought everything she wove.

With the money that the people paid for Thoni's weaving, Kori was soon a rich man. He built a big new house with many rooms and many windows. He bought herds of cattle and goats and other farm animals.

Kori was the happiest man. He had more than one name. His wife had a child that she could call her own. He was richer than he could ever have dreamed.

But Kori's wife was not happy.

She grew tired of Thoni's beauty. She grew tired of Thoni's mistakes. She even grew tired of Thoni's weaving.

"If only she could cook," she said to Kori. "If only she could milk the cows and feed the animals. If only she could do all the things other girls do for their mothers."

"She is different from other girls," Kori answered.

But his wife would not listen to his words.

"All she does is eat and weave," she went on.

"Always eating and weaving, weaving and eating. She does nothing else all day."

"She is only a child," Kori told her.

"Then why is she not like other children?" his wife asked angrily.

"Because she is not like other children. You know that. You know how long we waited for her. You know where she came from. Just thank God for what you have. There are many people who do not have half the things that Thoni has brought us."

All this was true. Kori's cattle were large. His herds were huge. His crops grew tall.

Kori's wife grew more and more angry.

"Thoni is lazy. She does not work in the fields. She does not watch over the animals."

"She weaves the most beautiful baskets," Kori said. "That is very hard work."

But Kori's wife grew more and more unhappy. And slowly, instead of loving Thoni, she started to change.

When Kori went out hunting, she would hit Thoni with a stick.

"And do not run to the gate to greet your father," she told the young girl. "Do not sing for him. Do not dance for him. Stay away from him."

"Why, mother, why? What have I done wrong?" Thoni asked.

"Everything," her mother answered. "You do everything wrong. And if you tell your father what I have said I shall throw you on the fire."

Thoni grew thin and ugly. Her beautiful black skin was rough and grey.

"Do you get enough to eat?" her father asked.

"Yes, father," she answered.

"Do you have pain?" he asked.

"No, father," she answered.

"Are you sick?" he asked.

"No father," she answered.

"Then tell me, dearest daughter, what is wrong. Why do you not sing and dance for me? Why do you not run to greet me?" Kori asked.

Thoni could not answer. She was too afraid.

# Chapter
# | 9 |

Kori did not know what was happening to Thoni, but he loved her dearly and wanted her to be well. He wanted to drive her sickness away.

He picked up his machete and went into the deep dark forest. When he came to the place where the oldest most sacred trees grew he stopped.

"God has led me to the sacred trees," he said to himself. "With God's help Thoni will live. Her sickness will go away."

He ran his fingers along his machete. It was sharp and bright.

"Please God, help me to save my child," he prayed.

Kori came home a few days later, tired but smiling. He carried a huge sack on his back. It was heavy with leaves and bark. He had picked the leaves from the sacred trees, and cut the bark himself with his machete.

"I shall make medicine for Thoni," he told his wife. "Her sickness will go away."

Kori put down the sack and his machete. His wife did not move.

"Light the fire. Boil water. You shall help me," he said to his wife.

Kori's wife did as she was told. She fetched wood and lit a great fire, but then she stood back. She watched Kori, but she would not help him.

Kori threw the leaves and the bark into a big pot. He boiled them on the fire for many hours. Then he added fat and honey, and left the pot to cool.

"You must drink this medicine," he told Thoni later. "Then you will be well again."

Thoni drank the medicine every morning and every night, but she did not get well. God did not answer Kori's prayers. The medicine did not help Thoni, for her sickness was not in her body.

Thoni grew thinner and thinner. Her beautiful long hair dropped out. Her eyes were dull. Her lovely white teeth turned yellow. She no longer smiled.

At last she lay down on a mat to wait for death. It was the saddest thing anyone had ever known.

Kori tried everything. He gave her more medicine. He sat with her and held her hand. He begged the wise men for help.

"I will give everything I have if you will save my daughter," he said. "I will give my goats. I will give my cattle. I will give all the money that I have. I will give anything to save Thoni."

It was no use. Thoni never smiled again. Kori was a sad and broken man.

One day Kori left to go hunting. He did not want to leave Thoni, but the family needed food.

Shortly after Kori left, something happened to his wife. Suddenly all the anger inside her could not be hidden any more.

She could not look at Thoni. She could not touch her or listen to her or speak to her.

She picked up Kori's machete and ran out into the yard.

"Burn, fire, burn," she screamed. Wildly she dug up the grass that Thoni used for her weaving and threw it on the fire. "Burn, fire, burn."

Thoni opened her tired eyes and watched. She saw the fire take hold until it nearly touched the sky. Then, as it died down, she slowly got up from her mat. She turned to Kori's wife and said, very quietly,

"I have been with you for many years. Now I am no longer wanted. I shall go back to my own people."

She did not say another word, or speak to Kori's wife again. Her work was finished. She washed herself, dressed, and tied back her hair.

When she was ready she took one last look at the hut where she had lived for so long.

"Tell my father I love him," she said softly, and walked away into the forest.

Kori's wife did not know what to do, or what to tell Kori when he came home. He started to ask questions at once.

"Where is Thoni? Did she drink the medicine? Has the sickness gone?"

His wife could not answer him. Kori guessed something was wrong.

"Tell me," he shouted. "Where is my daughter? Where is Thoni? What have you done to my child? What have you done to her?"

"She has gone," his wife screamed back. "Gone into the forest. Gone back to her own people. Gone for ever."

"What have you done, wife?" Kori waited. "Tell me."

Kori's wife told him what had happened, and how Thoni had walked away into the forest.

"Let her go," she finished. "She is no use here. She is lazy and does nothing right. She cannot cook. She cannot wash the clothes. She cannot watch over the cattle. She is no use. We do not need her. I do not want her any more. Let her go."

Kori did not listen to his wife. He only knew that his daughter had gone into the forest alone. And the forest was dangerous, full of snakes and wild animals.

"I must find her. I must find my daughter," he cried.

# Chapter
# 10

Kori picked up his spear and his arrows and ran into the forest after Thoni. He hurried along the path that she had taken. When he could, he ran. When he was tired, he walked. If he stopped he would never catch up with his daughter.

Kori went deeper and deeper into the forest, but he did not find Thoni.

For three days Kori pushed through the trees and tall grass, but he saw nothing and heard nothing. Then he looked down in the dust at his feet.

"Thoni stood here," he cried, "Thoni. Thoni. Where are you, Thoni?"

His own words, thrown back at him by the trees, were his only answer.

"Thoni. Thoni. Thoni."

Kori went on. He walked until he was so tired he could not stand. Then he called Thoni's name again.

"Thoni. Thoni. Thoni."

Again his own words were thrown back by the trees. "Thoni. Thoni. Thoni."
This was his only answer.

Still Kori would not give up. He pushed on through the darkest forests. He climbed the highest hills and went down into the deepest valleys. Every so often he would stop and sing this song out loud,

"Thoni, dear mother
Where are you, mother?
Answer your father
Do not go further."

There was never an answer, until one day he sang for the last time,

"Thoni, dear mother
Where are you, mother?
Answer your father
Do not go further."

He was almost ready to give up, but this time an answer came through the cold night air.

"Father, dear father
Let me go, I beg.
Your wife does not love me,
Says that I came from an egg
I am the child of a weaver."

When he heard this Kori was so angry that he could say no more. He took up his spear and his arrows and followed the song. He heard the words again and again.

"Father, dear father
Let me go, I beg.
Your wife does not love me,
Says that I came from an egg
I am the child of a weaver."

Kori travelled all night. The next morning, as the sun turned the dark sky to gold, he climbed out of the last deep valley. From the hill where he stood he could see many miles.

Far away, so far away that she looked tiny, he saw Thoni.

Kori started to run. He ran all morning, until the sun was hot, but Thoni was still far away. On and on he went, and by afternoon he was close enough to sing,
>"Thoni, Thoni, my mother
>Come back, mother.
>Listen to your father
>Do not go further."

Thoni did not answer, but hurried away. Kori ran after her.

Suddenly a great black cloud passed over Kori's head. He ran on, and then another cloud fell across his path. Then there was another, and then another still. Kori looked up – and all the sky was full of birds, thousands and thousands of screaming weaver birds.

Kori dropped his spear. This spear was his right arm, his right arm and his strength. It had never left his side before, but now he threw it away. He had to get to Thoni.

Then he threw away his arrows. These arrows were Kori's left arm, his meat and his honey. They had never left his side before, but now he threw them away too. He had to save Thoni.

Without his spear and his arrows Kori could run faster, but it was no good. The air was thick with weaver birds. There were so many that they hid the sun. They flew in a thousand great circles above his head. Their wings beat against his face and their sharp beaks cut into his body like knives.

Kori called out one last time,
>"Thoni, Thoni my mother
>Come back, mother.
>Listen to your father
>Do not go further."

# Chapter
## 11

Then Thoni looked back and saw her father.

He opened his arms to her, wanting her to come to him. She took three steps, trying to run to him. Then three huge birds screamed down from the sky, beaks open wide. Two of them took Thoni by the arms and carried her off, up and up into the air.

Kori tried to hold the legs of the third bird. It was a dusty old crow, as ugly as death. He held on for as long as he could, but then the crow broke free. It screamed one last time, and then flew away, up into the sky, after the others.

As suddenly as they had come, all the birds flew off. The sky was blue and the sun smiled down.

Kori was crying. Thoni had gone. He wanted his life to end. He cried for many hours and many days.

At last, tired and sad, Kori slept. When he opened his eyes and looked around he knew where he was. He had been to this place before. He had stood here before. Here he had dreamed a dream, the dream where the moon was broken.

There was nothing else for Kori to do. He sat very still for a long long time, and then he made his way home.

It was many days before Kori found his home again. When at last he walked out of the dark forest everything had changed. Everything was different.

His beautiful house, with all its doors and all its windows, had gone.

His crops had died in the fields.

His goats and his hens had gone.

His cattle had turned into wild animals and run away into the forest.

All the things Thoni had made, the mats and the baskets, had turned into grass.

His wife lay on the floor of her hut, old and tired and weak. She was dying from hunger. She had not eaten for many days.

No dreams ever came true again.

# Already available in **Mactracks**

*Starters*

**The Hunter's Dream**   Meja Mwangi
**Martha's Mistakes**   Lorna Evans
**Martha's Big News**   Lorna Evans
**Fiki Learns to Like Other People**   Lauretta Ngcobo
**Zulu Spear**   Olive Langa
**Mercy in a Hurry**   Mary Harrison
**Tanzai and Bube**   John Haynes
**Karabo's Accident**   Frances Cross
**The Little Apprentice Tailor**   Marcus Kamara
**Follow that Footprint!**   Jill Inyundo
**We're Still Moving!**   Damian Morgan

*Sprinters*

**Mystery of the Sagrenti Treasure**   Ekow Yarney
**Eyes and Ears**   Brenda Ferry
**Eyes and Ears Work Hard**   Brenda Ferry
**One in a Million**   Emma Johnson
**Map on the Wall**   Colin Swatridge
**Magic Trees**   Jenny Vincent
**Dark Blue is for Dreams**   Rosina Umelo
**Danger in the Palace**   Grace Nkansa
**Granny Sangoma**   John Byrne
**The Past Tells a Story**   Lorna Evans (*non-fiction*)

*Runners*

**Guitar Wizard**   Walije Gondwe
**Star**   Nandi Dlovu
**Days of Silence**   Rosina Umelo
**Never Leave Me**   Hope Dube
**Juwon's Battle**   Victor Thorpe
**Fineboy**   Maurice Sotabinda
**Front Page Story**   John Byrne
**Crocodile Challenge**   James Ngumy

*Winners*

**Halima**   Meshack Asare
**Foli Fights the Forgers**   Kofi Quaye
**Jojo in New York**   Kofi Quaye
**Presents from Mr Bakare**   Mary Harrison
**Sara's Friends**   Rosina Umelo
**Trouble in the City**   Hope Dube
**Sunbird's Paradise**   James Ngumy
**Kayo's House**   Barbara Kimenye
**Be Beautiful**   Lydia Eagle and Barbara Jackson (*non-fiction*)
**Sport in Africa**   Ossie Stuart (*non-fiction*)